# MONEY

14/9/2015.
Started writing in this book!

Julia B.

ALSO BY ARNOLD M. PATENT

*You Can Have It All*

*Money And Beyond*

*Bridges To Reality*

*The Treasure Hunt*

*The Journey*

# MONEY

### ARNOLD M. PATENT

Celebration Publishing
*Tucson, Arizona*

Celebration Publishing
230 South Palace Gardens Drive
Tucson, AZ 85748

Text and cover design by
Kaelin Chappell Broaddus

Library of Congress Control Number: 2004118139
ISBN-13: 978-0-9708081-4-1
ISBN-10: 0-9708081-4-3

First Printing March 2005
Printed in the United States of America
Printed in the United Kingdom

To my dear wife
*Selma*
who showers me with
love and support every day

## ACKNOWLEDGMENTS

To Betty and Frank McElhill
for handling office and other details
with love, care and generosity

To Grady Claire Porter
for supporting me in
accepting and appreciating
who I really am

# CONTENTS

# INTRODUCTION

"It's a baby boy!" I was born in 1929—the year of the stock market crash—into a three generation household headed initially by my mother's father, a prosperous businessman. By 1939, my grandfather was worn out, beaten down and ashamed after losing his battle to stave off bankruptcy of a company he started and owned for 30 years. He handed over financial responsibility for the family to my father who was working long hours to build his law practice.

This was my basis for the belief that money came after a lot of struggle and hard work as well as the belief that holding onto money was almost impossible. I was convinced that there was nothing simple or easy about having money.

Certain about the way the money game worked, I set out on my own as a practicing lawyer repeating the patterns of behavior I witnessed growing up.

I worked hard to bring money in and struggled against having to let it go. I also had a lot of hidden anger at having to work so hard for money. By keeping the supply limited, I could avoid being generous —an indirect way to express the anger.

Little did I realize that these events and circumstances were carefully orchestrated to instill in me a very precise way to relate to money.

After many years of recreating the experiences with money that were modeled for me by my family during my early years, an inner voice spoke to me. I called what I heard Universal Principles[1]. The very first one was the Principle of Abundance. Abundance is the natural state of the Universe.

I knew the truth of these Principles as soon as I heard them. The power of this truth motivated me to share the Principles with anyone who would listen.

At first I was invited to speak to small groups in living rooms. This rapidly expanded to large groups at weekend seminars, and a few years later to the publishing of a book called *You Can Have It All.*

Although I spent almost two decades speaking and writing about the Principles, my personal experience with money remained the same. The Principle of Abundance and my personal experience with money stayed on separate tracks.

My frustration with the failure to use my understanding of the Principles to influence my experience with money inspired me to open for more support. This led to the opportunity to receive spiritual coaching.

[1]Appendix D, Page 76

I have written about this awareness-expanding experience in *The Journey*. The most surprising awareness was that I was the creator of every experience of my life, not just a participant. As for money, I was the one who gave it power and convinced myself that I was powerless without it.

At the time I wrote *The Journey*, I did not realize how much power I had vested in money. I continued with the coaching and not only uncovered many ways I hid power in money, but also how intricately I wove money into my other creations. I also used this support to reclaim a lot of the power I had placed in money and thereby enjoy more of the abundance of my natural state.

*Money* is my way of sharing my expanded awareness and experience.

## CHAPTER 1

# Our Natural State and Our Human State

Who are we? We are the Power and Presence of God. We are a consciousness of Oneness that is in perfect harmony, joyful, all-knowing, infinitely abundant and all-powerful.

Using our unlimited power, we create our human state. This is an experience that is different from and in most ways opposite to our natural state. Having a totally different experience is the purpose of this unique adventure.

We can compare the creation of the human experience to that of creating a game such as baseball or monopoly. The games are based on a concept and rules and regulations. The games work as long as the concept, rules and regulations are accepted and followed.

The way that the human game is different from any other game is the extraordinary complexity and variety of the concepts, rules and regulations that form the basis for the game.

We also create a human persona to play the human game. The purpose of the human persona is to hide who we really are.

The vehicle we use to create the human game (and the human persona as player) is called a belief. A belief is an idea (a concept) we make up and that we accept as true.

Since our natural state is Oneness, we create beliefs that make us seem separate from each other. Since our natural state is perfect harmony, we create beliefs that make chaos, challenge and stress seem real. Since our natural state is joy, we create beliefs that make anger, sadness, anxiety and loneliness seem real. Since our natural state is all-knowing, we create beliefs that convince us that we know very little and must be educated. Since we are infinitely abundant, we create beliefs that shortage and limitation are real. Since we are all-powerful, we create beliefs that there is power in other people, institutions and circumstances and that our power is limited.

What is important to remember is that the human experience is all made up. It is a creature of imagination. The human experience is like a movie—images on a screen that entertain us but have no reality.

Creating the human experience is an extraordinary accomplishment. We have made up something so extensive, so varied, so challenging and demanding and so engrossing that we have become addicted to it. I see this as a game that we love to play.

This game that we have accepted as real acts as a veil of challenge, struggle, stress, fear and limitation placed over our consciousness of Oneness that remains in its natural sate of perfect harmony and infinite abundance.

We experience everything through our consciousness. Our consciousness is our Infinite Intelligence, the God Presence, the Soul Self that we are.

This Presence is an energy—the sole energy in the Universe—unconditional love. This energy is like clay; we mold it with a belief, into anything we wish. However, whatever we create is still energy. Its apparent reality in physical form is just an illusion.

Money is one of these creations. The beliefs we have about money are extensive. Since money plays such a dominant role in our lives, I have used it to support the reader in appreciating that the consciousness we use in dealing with money determines our experience with it.

## CHAPTER 2

# Beliefs, Judgments and Consequences

As mentioned previously, the vehicle we use to play with energy is belief—another word for concept. A belief is created in our consciousness. A belief has whatever importance we say it has.

The whole human experience is based on concepts, created in our fertile imaginations. After crafting the concepts and hiding power in them so that they seem real, we require something to keep the power hidden.

We have assigned this role to judgment—the do's and don'ts, rights and wrongs of human behavior. When we judge something we lock the energy in whatever we judge. This means that we keep experiencing whatever we are judging precisely the way we judge it to be.

However, the concept of judgment is meaningless without the concept of consequences. Suffering the consequences of violating rules of behavior gives the rules their impact.

Each of us, as the Power and Presence of God, creates the concepts and consequences of our own human experience. In other words, each of us establishes the rules, the punishment for the violation, and then enforces the punishment upon himself. And what is most fascinating is that the concepts and consequences exist only in our consciousness.

Judging something does not change what it really is—unconditional love.

The sole purpose of creating a belief is to disguise our natural state. The new game we are ready to play is reclaiming the power we have placed in our beliefs—the building blocks of our physical world. This game is played in consciousness where our true power resides.

On the following page, and at other places in the book, you will have the opportunity to list your beliefs.

## List Some Beliefs You Have Created
*Example: I do not have enough money*

~~I want to earn big bucks → $100 000 a year~~

1. I don't know if I'll ever have sufficient money to not work but still maintain my current std of living.
2. I'll need to work till I'm 70+ before this might be possible.
3. I have to rely on my self to do this.
4. I cannot rely on others to do this for me - guide me to wealth!
5. I am afraid to expose myself to public scrutiny. I will be found wanting. I don't know enuf/anythg.!
6. I am afraid of being on my own in my old age.
7. I am nervous about trusting life.

## List the Feelings You Have About Each Belief
*Example: frustration, disappointment and shame*

1. Frustration. Fear.
2. Impatience. Uncertainty.
3. Fear.
4. Fear.
5. Not good enough!
6. Fear.
7. Uncertain. Fear.

Can you see how the beliefs and the descriptions of the feelings are also judgments?

## List of Other Judgments You Hold

*Example: Some people have too much money and some too
little*

1. Poor people only have themselves to blame.
2. I am envious of rich people. Don't like the bling + childishness I see in a lot of them. My relative wealth feels comfortable + I'm not 'too' rich or 'too' poor. (??).
3. Making money is RISKY! I could lose everything!

## List the Feelings You Have About Each Judgment

*Example: annoyed and angry*

1. Anger.
2. Frustration. Self satisfied.
3. Fear / judgment. Big fear!

## List the Consequences You Have Created for Each Belief

*Example: People do not respect me*

I cannot be poor. Cannot real myself. Poor people are themselves to blame! Shame! Old age - fear! Too much risk!

To earn a good salary is less risky.

Comfort of being in the fold - regular pay check.

Do what I can with that.

Being real entails personal exposure.

I can't real expose myself publicly.

Exposure will show me up as a fraud,

I don't know if I care enough about people to carry it through to a conclusion, and do it long term.

I don't want power over people.

I don't want control of peoples lives.

I don't want their lives in my hands.

I can't save them.

I don't want to be responsible for other peoples lives.

This feels too risky

## Trace A Belief Through Different Parts of Your Life And Find The Common Element

*Example: I do not have enough money. I am not smart enough. I am not successful enough in my career. I am not good looking enough. The common element is "I Am Not Enough."*

I am an odd ball.
I get overly involved in topics of personal interest.
What I have to say is not that interesting.
My spiritual search is just for me.
I wouldn't presume to help anyone else. I'm not that interesting. Not sure that I'm interested.

I AM NOT ENOUGH.
(even Now!) Since A LOAD OF THOUGHT TO SEE THROUGH!

I don't want to be interested — I may become responsible.
This is too risky. don't want to carry another

load.

I have created the following test to bring to your attention some of the ways you may have given importance and power to money.

## A TEST

1. Do you believe that it is better to spend as little as possible for something you are purchasing? *(Yes)*

2. Do you pay close attention to how much money you have? *(Yes)*

3. Are you concerned about having enough money to support yourself? *(Yes)*

4. Are you careful about spending money? *(Yes)*

5. Do you try to save money? *(Yes)*

6. Do you feel that your life is limited by how much money you have? *(Yes)*

If your answer to any of these questions is yes, you know you have invested money with power. It is evidence that you have succeeded in creating what you set out to create—making your human experience of limitation seem real.

Whatever is present in our lives is evidence that we have a total commitment to have it there just the way it is. This is also evidence of how focused, persevering and creative we are. These are qualities to appreciate.

Appreciation for whatever disguises are present in our lives, as well as appreciation for us as the creators of them is an integral part of the process of reclaiming the power we have vested in the creations.

## CHAPTER 3

# Money Is Energy

The disguises (beliefs) we have attached to money are among our most stellar achievements. Around the pure loving energy that money is, we have wrapped beliefs such as shortage, obligation, hard work, loss, manipulation, security and survival. We have then wrapped layers of emotional consequences such as fear, frustration, anger and shame.

When money is seen and felt as love, we enjoy using it to express our naturally loving qualities of generosity and appreciation. The more we use money to express appreciation, the more money flows in support of this expression and our natural state of abundance becomes more of our reality.

## List Beliefs You Have About Money

I am pretty good at saving money. A bit fearful that it will go away + will lose all.

I would love to have millions (of pounds). I would love to experience that kind of abundance.

There's a sneaky belief that earning mega bucks comes via dishonesty. I want to maintain integrity — Rafael has happy with his!

I love quality — but will spend less — sometimes not quite as good. dont always give myself the best (try).

I need to SAVE to ensure I can live comfortably in my old(er) age.

It feels right that life is truly abundant —> but it eludes me + I dont know how to see that clearly — or how to achieve it.

## List Feelings You Have About Each Belief

Fraid / Frustrated that I dont know how to do better. Unsure of decisions in good/bad times.

Joy! Would love to!

If I remain where I am, I'll be 'safe' — all aspects of legal duties are fulfilled.

Bemused.

Why. I dont spend consciously any more — I always leave excess + shove it to SAVINGS as + when.

Would like to do better with SAVINGS.

Would like to see money flow toward me in a steady/sure way.

13

# CHAPTER 4

# God — The Oneness

In order to create our human experience, we have made God into the ultimate authority figure. She stands in judgment of everything we think and do. She rewards good deeds and punishes bad ones.

What is crucial for us to recognize is that how we perceive God determines how we experience our lives. We always project our beliefs onto the world around us. This is another way of saying that we always experience an outplaying of the state of our own consciousness.

It is only when we know and feel that each of us is a God Presence that we can trust that every experience we have is really loving, joyful and abundant no matter how it appears.

## CHAPTER 5

# Security

Security is a feeling, and it comes from within us. It is an acceptance of who we really are.

Insecurity is a sense of vulnerability that arises from giving power to the physical world. The purpose of this creation is to make insecurity and vulnerability seem real. And, we have succeeded. In this vulnerable, fearful state our major concerns—poverty, pain and death—seem real to us.

With our focus on the physical world as real, we treat it as our nemesis rather than the disguise of our true power and abundance.

## CHAPTER 6

# The Body

The body is the vehicle we use to relate to the physical world.

The body and the physical world justify each other's existence. Without the physical world, our body has no purpose. Without our body, the physical world has no purpose.

As stated previously, both exist only in our consciousness. But what a brilliant consciousness we have that creates these remarkable toys for the playground we call our human experience.

As part of the creation, we endowed the body with intelligence. However, the body's intelligence is as much of an illusion as the body is. All intelligence resides in our consciousness—the Infinite Intelligence of the God Presence that we are.

When we consider our security, we are really talking about the security of our body. How do we secure the body? We secure the body by providing it with sufficient food, clothing, shelter and a safe environment.

This is where money comes in. Money is the tool to provide what we consider necessary to keep us secure.

However, money in this context is as much of an illusion as the rest of our physical reality. We cannot create security for our body with money or anything else.

We created our bodies to experience insecurity, one of the many limitations of our human experiences that we have convinced ourselves are real.

The creation of our bodies is a miraculous accomplishment. Upon reflection, we can appreciate that nothing less than a miraculous intelligence can create something with so many extraordinary features. This intelligence is our Infinite Intelligence — the Guide for our journey through this human experience.

Having used our bodies to play here subject to the many limitations we have created and accepted as real, we now have the opportunity to enjoy playing here in these same bodies free of these limitations. We access this freedom by appreciating ourselves as the miraculous beings we truly are — the Power and Presence of God — the creator of our bodies and all of the many ways we experience them.

CHAPTER 7

# Abundance

Abundance is our natural state. When shortage or limitation seems present in our lives, it is because we have created a belief to make that seem true. This is the signal to remind ourselves: that all power, all abundance is already ours; that we are looking at a situation we have created to make our human experience of limitation seem real.

There is brilliance in our ability to create a persona that is needy, limited in many ways and often a victim of people and circumstances that are more powerful. Yet, rather than appreciate ourselves for this extraordinary accomplishment, we either overlook it, or continue to see ourselves as powerless in the face of forces beyond our control.

The avoidance of Self-appreciation is not accidental; it is intentional. There is great power in our natural state of Self-appreciation. In order for us to successfully create our human experience, we have had to be certain that this strong energy of Self-appreciation is well hidden.

This is why we have created so many beliefs that discourage us from feeling Self-appreciation: we call it arrogance, lack of humility, pride, self-interest, self-importance and selfishness.

We have given these terms meanings opposite to Self-appreciation and have accepted these meanings as real as a way of keeping our Self-appreciation hidden.

What is true Self-appreciation? It is appreciation for one's Self that includes all selves. Self-appreciation is appreciation for the Oneness, the God Presence that we are.

Arrogance, lack of humility, pride, self-interest, self-importance and selfishness are intentionally defined to exclude others and thus act as a disguise for our natural state of Self-appreciation.

The good news is that locating a disguise tells us we are right in our true power. We can never change who we really are. The solution is to stop calling what we are feeling by the disguise and call it what it really is.

This is challenging because what we are feeling as the disguise is uncomfortable and seems contrary to what is being disguised. For example: self-interest feels different from Self-appreciation.

However, this is evidence of our ingenuity in convincing ourselves that the concepts of arrogance, lack of humility, pride, self-interest, self-importance and selfishness are real.

We are now ready for the next step — accepting the different feeling as an expansion of what the feeling really is. For example: let the feeling we associate with self-interest be an expansion of the feeling we associate with Self-appreciation even though it seems uncomfortable.

We consider the feeling uncomfortable only because we have convinced ourselves that it is. Being in an energy that we call uncomfortable is a gift, not a punishment. We are right in the presence of our real power of Self-appreciation. We can now embrace the energy as what it really is and reclaim the power we have hidden there.

Feeling appreciation is the first part of an experience that is completed when we express that appreciation. This is where money comes in. The sole purpose of money is to express appreciation.

In addition to abundance being our natural state, so is the feeling of appreciation. The more appreciation we express, the more money we allow to flow in our lives to support that expression. This is how we enjoy the abundance that is always present.

## CHAPTER 8

# Appreciation

Appreciation is the ever-expanding energy of valuing. Appreciation is the joyful expression of acceptance of one's Self as the Oneness. In the human, the act of true appreciation is the greatest gift we give ourselves. Affording others the opportunity to appreciate extends and expands this gift.[1]

This is illustrated by a friend's experience at a dinner party she made for her daughter and her daughter's friends. In appreciation for the dinner invitation the daughter's friends brought the host and her daughter a dozen roses and other gifts. Generosity begets generosity.

Compared with most people in the world, those

[1] This is an excerpt from a Grady Claire Porter meditation, APPRECIATION; the full text is in Appendix C on page 68.

reading this book are appreciably better off. We have more freedom, more opportunities and more material wealth. Yet our underlying emotion is one of insecurity and fear. We believe that there is not enough for everyone and that only those who are aggressive and competitive win out.

The general acceptance of a world of shortage results in a paradoxical response. Instead of appreciating all that so many of us do have, we take for granted what we have and worry endlessly about what we do not have. In addition, we act in ways that are very illogical and imprudent for people who accept that shortage is a fact of life. We run up large debts and borrow heavily against those things we do have—our houses or our incomes.

What is most devastating about this irrational response is the depressed feeling quality that comes in its wake. Many people are exhausted from fighting this battle known as "keeping ahead."

What I have just described seems so real because we have created that reality. This creation is purposeful, for without it, our human experience is not possible.

We have used all of our formidable power, creativity, imagination and ingenuity to make the challenges of our life seem real. These same qualities are available to us to reclaim the power we have hidden in these challenges.

A way to start reclaiming our power is to:

1. Appreciate the creation of the disguises that hide our power;

2. Appreciate making the disguises seem so real;

3. Appreciate making these disguises so annoying, frustrating and painful that we stay away from them with a passion; and

4. Appreciate all that we presently have.

Appreciation is an aspect of love. It is a powerful focus that cuts through the confusion and chaos of our self-created perception of life as a scary struggle for survival. Whenever we allow ourselves to feel appreciation for anything, our hearts open and we connect a little more deeply to our God Presence and the unlimited abundance of our natural state.

From a practical standpoint, why have anything if, when having it, we deny ourselves the greatest benefit we can possibly derive from it? The benefit is the joyful feeling of appreciation and the opportunity to express that appreciation to expand the value of all that we have.

## CHAPTER 9

# The Gift of Self-Appreciation

Reaching a state of Self-appreciation is the ultimate gift we give ourselves. Self-appreciation is the knowing that all power is within us. Self-appreciation comes from loving ourselves so completely that we see and feel others only through that love. In a state of Self-appreciation, Oneness is our reality.

Whatever we experience is always a reflection of the state of our consciousness: a projection of how we see ourselves. When I feel worried or concerned about someone, I know I am seeing a reflection of worry or concern I feel for myself. If I am free of worry and concern, another person cannot stimulate these emotions in me. What I see in them is a reflection of the God Presence that I have accepted as my reality.

When a person appears powerless and victimized, I

realize that she is reflecting my belief that we are separate from the God Presence, the Oneness. If I accept this presentation as real, I strengthen my belief of separateness, powerlessness and victimization.

An example is a person begging on a street corner. Accepting this display of poverty as real, I sympathize with the beggar. But sympathy is the opposite of Self-appreciation. Sympathy accepts the separateness and powerlessness as real. Self-appreciation is the knowing that I am never separate or powerless. Self-appreciation allows me to connect directly with the God Presence of the beggar, feel his true power, and trust his choice to fully experience the role of beggar. I am then free to decide, without the sense of obligation that accompanies sympathy, whether or not to offer material support.

When we feel Self-appreciation, we are expressing our deep trust in the unconditional love and support of the Universe. There is nothing more joyful and fulfilling than a state of deep Self-appreciation. Self-appreciation is for the Wholeness, the God Presence that we are. This is appreciation that embraces all that we see and experience. This is a state of knowing that there is nothing outside of us; that we are the whole of this unconditionally loving and supportive Universe.

## List of Qualities You Have That You Appreciate

*Example: loyal, dependable, honest, talented*

*insightful . Conscienscious . Intrigued . Caring . Loving . Open .*
*Honest . Forthright . Careful . Thoughtful . Intent . Focussed .*
*Talented . Bright . Independent . Self Sufficient .*

## List of Qualities You Have that You Don't Appreciate

*Example: lazy, rigid, timid, unfocused*

*Forgetful . dramatic . Cry a lot .*

Are you willing to embrace in unconditional love those qualities you don't appreciate each time one of them comes to your attention until they become creations you consider worthy of appreciation?

## CHAPTER 10

# Unconditional Love

We feel our connection with our God Presence, the Wholeness, through our open hearts. The more open our hearts, the deeper our connection to our God Presence and the more powerful we feel.

The God Presence that we are is the purity, joyfulness and magnificence of unconditional love. In order to create the reality of our human experience (the opposite of our natural state), we have devised the concept of conditional love: unless certain conditions are met, love is not deserved or warranted. Having used the unlimited creative power of our imagination to make conditional love seem real, that is what we experience.

Some examples of conditional love include: a parent requiring a child to do homework before he can watch television, or clean up his room before he can play with his friends; an employer requiring an employee to produce a certain quantity of new orders before he receives a raise; or a citizen requiring a candidate to vote in favor of gun control to gain her vote.

There are an endless number of examples of conditions we encounter every day, since the whole human experience is based on conditional love and conditional acceptance.

The magnificence of our real Self, the pure consciousness that is the Power and Presence of God, is something to be deeply appreciated. When we feel this deep appreciation, our Being is filled with joyfulness. In order for our human experiences to seem real, we have had to disguise this feeling of joy.

This brings us to one of our most imaginative disguises: MONEY. The power we have vested in it, and the many conditions we have to meet to have use of it has hidden a lot of joy. The conditions we have created around money include having to work hard to bring it in, having to spend it carefully so that there is enough left over for unexpected expenses such as illness and expected challenges such as old age and retirement.

When we reclaim the power we have vested in money, money returns to its natural state—unconditional love—the energy of our true Self that we deeply appreciate. As unconditional love, money assumes its unique role in our lives: a vehicle to express the appreciation that fills our Being.

As with unconditional love, appreciation expands when we express it. This is true of money as the vehicle with which we express appreciation: the more we use money to express appreciation, the more money flows to us to express appreciation with.

The appreciation we express is always for ourselves. Though it seems that there are "others" who are the recipients, they are just imaginative creations to support us in playing the human game of limitation. We have created them to support us in making believe that there are justifications to withhold money or to give it out in limited amounts since our supply is limited.

The opportunity we have is to reclaim the power in all the conditions and judgments we have about money. The first step is to acknowledge that the conditions and judgments are self created: whatever limitations or challenges we are experiencing with money are our creations. And, they are brilliant creations. Remember, we are the Power and Presence of God who have convinced ourselves that we are mere powerless mortals who have to work hard to bring money in, and have to be careful that we control its departure so that we will have enough left over to sustain ourselves in a difficult and unsafe world.

As we reclaim the power we have placed in money and the conditional ways it moves in our lives, we notice that we feel ever-growing trust in unconditional love—the Power and Presence of God that we are—and in our natural state of abundance.

CHAPTER 11

# Expanding Our Awareness

As we expand our awareness of who we really are, we recognize that:

1. Conditions and judgments are totally subjective experiences on our part.

2. We interpret people's behavior based on our belief system.

3. We are not at the effect of another.

4. We are not victims in the money game.

5. There is no power outside of us.

However, having created the belief that we are victims, we dutifully make believe that we are, and continue the game of conditional love.

A condition is a judgment. When we judge a person

as not being perfect just the way she is, we justify withholding love from that person. We invariably see the judgment as being the result of something the other person has said or done. What we overlook is that it is our interpretation of the words spoken or the act performed that gives rise to the judgment.

Our presence on this planet is an opportunity to open the energy around and free ourselves of the many conditions we have created to make our human experience possible. To take advantage of this opportunity, we remember that we have chosen these conditions and the judgments. We have chosen the parents, siblings, relatives, friends and associates who generate the precise conditions that we now find so challenging. We also have chosen the judgmental way we interpret their behavior.

Once we accept this broader view, we move to the next step, which is opening our hearts and feeling our feelings fully, freely and unconditionally. As we continue in this process, we lose more of our investment in the power of conditions. Our love becomes increasingly unconditional, and that unconditional love is reflected back to us from those we interact with.

In connecting with our true power, the power of unconditional love, we place money in a new perspective. We accept that money, like everything else in the material world, is a reflection of the state of our consciousness. We accept that money flows freely in our lives when we allow it to. We also accept that when money isn't flowing freely, we have given importance to some preconceived condition.

Unconditional love is the real game of life. It is the way we connect to the power that we truly are. It is also the doorway to our natural environment of total freedom and unlimited abundance.

## CHAPTER 12

# Consciousness

Our consciousness is the all-knowing, all-powerful Presence that we are. We often refer to it as our Infinite Intelligence. Our consciousness is always present and active in us. Our consciousness creates the events and circumstances that provide us with perfect support. That includes bringing us face-to-face with the events or circumstances where we have hidden our power.

What is important to remember is that the events and circumstances in our lives are present because we have created them. However, they are just in our imagination. We give them the illusion of power by making believe that the power we have placed in them is real. We then treat the illusion of power as real so that we have a game to play. The games we play make up our human experience.

What seems like the worst place to be is really the best place to be. The discomfort we feel (such as shame, anger and fear) is the disguise for a power that we have hidden. We reclaim the power by embracing the disguise as what it really is—the Power and Presence of God.

Often we avoid feeling our feelings because we believe the process is too painful. Instead, we use our intellects to attempt to resolve the situation without realizing that the sole purpose for creating the situation is to bring up the feelings so that we can reclaim the power we have hidden.

Many of us are so sophisticated in using our intellects to avoid feeling our feelings that our intellects have become defense mechanisms that we employ to keep our feelings at bay.

Instead of judging ourselves for using our intellects, we can appreciate how effective this approach has been in keeping us away from where our power is hidden. Remember, this is what we set out to accomplish. If we hadn't successfully hidden our power and kept it hidden, our human experience would not have been possible.

The extensive use of our intellects in dealing with money tells us that we have placed power in money, are feeling the loss of that power and thus have reason to feel fearful and insecure.

Feeling fearful and insecure about money is the signal that we are feeling the power of our true Self.

What we are calling fear and insecurity is the power disguised by names we made up to hide the power. We are right in the perfect place to reclaim the power we have hidden in money.

## CHAPTER 13

# Core Beliefs

What have we covered in the preceding chapters? We are Divine Beings—pure, unconditionally loving and all-powerful. We are deeply appreciative of this extraordinary Self. Choosing to play the game we call our human experience, we have to hide both the power of this Divine Being and the power of appreciation that we feel for it. We accomplish this by using the ingenuity of this Self to create disguises—beliefs—that convince us we are unworthy and undeserving of appreciation.

Since these beliefs (and the feelings they give rise to) hide an enormous amount of power, I refer to them as core beliefs. One of my core beliefs has been that I have to make a lot of money to be successful. I also made sure that I didn't meet this expectation so that I could feel a sense of embarrassment for this failure.

I committed myself to keep the need to be successful and the certainty of failure as one game I came to play in the human. My human experience became a series of events that kept reminding me of my failure, thus triggering constant feelings of shame.

What I call shame is the disguise for the Power and Presence of God that I hid in shame. The amazing part of this is how I was able to convince myself that I am less than who I really am. This starts with the creation of concepts such as success, failure and shame followed by total acceptance of these concepts as real even though they exist only in my imagination.

I accomplished this remarkable feat because the power of my creativity is so great that I can make something with no reality seem real. This vesting of power in concepts creates the illusion of power in something outside that can limit, oppose, diminish or harm me.

Placing power outside provided me with a rich source of people to complain about and find fault with. The first volunteers I invited to fill these roles were my parents, relatives, teachers and other influential figures I interacted with during my early years. They are the many people who agreed, at my request, to follow the script written for the play I call my human experience—my intentional creation of a world of limitation.

Even though I have convinced myself otherwise, my natural state of unlimited joy, enthusiasm, creativity, freedom and abundance is always present waiting for me to accept and appreciate. I do that by first accepting and appreciating that I am the brilliant creator of the core beliefs that disguise my natural state and then appreciating the creation of the core beliefs themselves.

Until I am able to accept that I am the source of power, that I am the creator of all that I see and experience, the power remains where I have placed it—in the dangerous and scary world I live in.

This is why I have committed myself to appreciating the incredible accomplishment of making a seeming reality of my powerlessness in the face of a world of enormous power when, in fact, I am the Power and Presence of God and there is no power outside of me.

This brings me back to the process of reclaiming the power hidden in my core beliefs. As stated previously, the Power of God that I am is enormous and thus the energy hidden in my core concepts is enormous. Reclaiming this power means going into these intense energies and embracing them as what they really are. Maintaining awareness of the following truths is helpful to the opening of this vast storehouse of energy:

I am, at all times, unconditionally loved and supported by the Universe and all in It; and

I am, at all times, free to accept and appreciate this gift of unconditional love and feel it for my magnificent and Divine Self.

My parents and all the other people in my formative years, who, at my request, volunteered to play the roles I asked of them, remain my partners on this journey. As long as I blame and resent them, they mirror my withholding of deep unconditional love and appreciation from my Self. When I reclaim the power I have vested in making the feelings of blame and resentment seem real, these same people mirror back the deep unconditional love and appreciation I feel for my Self by expressing that love and appreciation for me freely and joyfully.

When I made a commitment to reclaim the power hidden in my core beliefs, perfect support appeared to guide me through the process. I know, without doubt, that the whole Universe mirrors my deep commitment to expand my appreciation for who I really am and for all my creations.

## CHAPTER 14

# Money and Core Beliefs

A core belief, as I have already stated, is one that has a lot of power hidden in it. I vested a lot of power in money: power to provide me with food, shelter and clothing; power to bring me security; power to bring me success; power to give me status and importance in my community, and the power to provide me with the pleasures of life. With all this power placed in it, money certainly qualifies as a core belief.

Seen as pieces of paper, money has no intrinsic value. All of the power money has comes from vesting power in it.

Why did I give power to money? For the same reason I have given power to anything: to give a sense of reality to the game I call my human experience. Without my vesting power in something, it doesn't exist for me.

When I place a large amount of power in some thing or some one, I feel and act as though I am dependent upon the recipient of the power. Having placed so much of my power in money, I spent a huge amount of time and energy trying to acquire money in order to recover the power I felt that I didn't have without money. Looked at from this perspective, what I did does not seem very intelligent.

However, there is another perspective to consider: If I had retained all of the power in who I really am—the Power and Presence of God—there is no human game. Since I have come here to play the human game, hiding power in money, and the creation of the money game is an ingenious way to make the human game seem real.

As a result of placing power in money, I diminished my power and trust in the Principle of Abundance: Abundance is my natural state. Instead, I experienced the corollary to the Principle: If I am experiencing less than total abundance in each and every aspect of my life, it means that I am literally pushing abundance away.

This Principle and its corollary remind me that it takes an activist position to keep money out. When money isn't present in my life, I can be sure I am in a state of active resistance.

I set up a state of active resistance by creating beliefs that I had to make a lot of money to be successful and then making sure that I didn't so that I seemed to be a failure. When I look at the patterns I created around money, I see how I kept a lid on how much I allowed myself to bring in. This was not obvious at first because of the ingenious ways I kept my intention to keep a lid on money hidden from myself. This is all part of the ingenuity and commitment it takes to disguise my real Self in the imaginative creation of my human self.

With the support I created to guide me through the process, I heightened my awareness to the concepts I created and the clever ways I made them real for me. The most challenging part of the process is dealing with the many judgments I have about the events and circumstances I face every day.

Having accepted failure as real and feeling the shame I associated with failure, I carried this shame as a burden. This is something I wanted to rid myself of. However, judging something acts to keep it in place.

The dilemma then becomes on the one hand seeing the judgment as made up, and on the other hand appreciating the need to maintain the reality of the judgment to keep my human experience in place. In the constant throes of having to succeed and seeing failure and feeling shame, this situation seemed anything but made up.

For many years when I felt the discomfort of feeling shame for not having enough money, I worked hard to bring in more money to alleviate the uncomfortable feeling.

Improving a situation so that I feel better assumes that what I am fixing is real. However, everything I experience is something I made up and have convinced myself is real. My human experiences start and remain in my imagination.

I can't fix something that is fictitious. When I try, I reinforce its seeming reality. This expands the source of discomfort rather than reducing it.

Aware of the futility of trying to change or eliminate the feeling of shame, I embrace the feeling of shame as what it really is—the disguise for the joyful feeling of appreciating the abundant being I really am.

No matter how many beliefs I create to disguise my natural state of abundance, and I have created many of them, I know that I cannot alter or diminish my natural state. I keep reminding myself that my abundance is present right here and right now. I also keep reminding myself that expressing appreciation for my abundance is one of my greatest joys.

## CHAPTER 15

# Want

Placing power in money is how we hide the power of abundance that is our natural state. Creating the concept of "want" is a clever way we keep the power hidden.

The brilliance in the creation of this concept is that "wanting" something confirms to us that we do not already have it. In our natural state of abundance everything is already ours. Every time we increase our focus on "wanting" something, we reassure ourselves it is not already ours.

By believing it is not already ours, we make that belief our experience—we keep money out of reach. This is why surveys that ask people how much more money they require to have "enough" report the same response irrespective of a person's present financial condition. Almost everyone questioned answers 20 to

25 percent more than they have. Wanting more insures that we never have enough.

We have devised another way to keep our power hidden in money. We judge the money game we have created. The frustration, struggle and anxiety we feel when we play the money game and the seeming inequality amongst the players insures that we are in a constant state of judgment of the game. The Principle of Nonjudgment tells us that when we judge anything, we keep experiencing it just the way we judge it to be.

This brings us to the sole purpose of money: to experience and express appreciation. Conversely, the sole purpose of the money game is to hide our experience and expression of appreciation.

What are we appreciating? We are appreciating our Self, who we are—the Power and Presence of God—and our natural state of unlimited abundance.

As described above, the creation of the money game and the many ways we have kept the game going has served its intended purpose.

Every time we reclaim more of the power we have hidden in money, we free more of the feeling of appreciation for our Self and the joy we feel when we express this appreciation with money.

Since we relate to everyone based on how we see our Self, we cannot over-emphasize the importance of feeling appreciation for our Self. We cannot feel too much appreciation. Everything we experience is something we have created so that we may enjoy the activity of creation. There are no "bad" or "mistaken" creations. Remember, there is no power in our creations. All power remains in us all of the time.

Creating a shortage of money, considering our Self a failure and feeling ashamed are amazing creations when we consider that we are The Power and Presence of God making believe we are short of money and a failure.

Everything we create is part of the abundance of life. When we avoid appreciating anything we create, we literally withhold abundance from our Self.

We are masters of withholding abundance from our Self. This is the way we make our human experiences of limitation seem real. In retracing the ways we hide the power of appreciation for our Self and our natural state of abundance, we become aware of how ingenious we are.

This brings us to an important step we can take to reclaim the enormous power in Self-appreciation: devote some time to appreciate how brilliantly we have hidden this power in one of our most imaginative creations—the money game.

When we reclaim the power hidden in the money game:

We free money to be an expression of love and appreciation;

We expand the love and appreciation we feel for

our Self that is then reflected back to us as expressions of love and appreciation from those around us; and

We become aware that we experience the expression of appreciation in the same way we experience the expression of love. The expression of love fills our being with even more love to express. The expression of appreciation (with money) fills our being with even more appreciation to express and the money with which to express it.

## CHAPTER 16

# The Purpose of Beliefs, Events and Circumstances

The initial purpose of the creation of our beliefs and the events and circumstances that reflect them is to disguise who we are so that our human experience comes into existence. This is the phase when we hide the power of unconditional love, harmony, joy and abundance of our natural state.

When we are ready to reclaim this power, our Infinite Intelligence creates events and circumstances to arouse within us feelings of discomfort to show us where we have hidden our power.

The events and circumstances of our day have no other meaning or importance. Winning the lottery is not a "good" creation and being short of money to pay the rent is not a "bad" creation. They are both imaginary creations. The "bad" ones are not to be fixed or

made better. Every creation, just the way it is, is perfect for the purpose of supporting us in reclaiming
the power we have hidden in the feelings that are
aroused.

## List of Creations You Consider Wonderful
*Example: Had dinner at your favorite restaurant*

*Powerful cars. My gorgeous flat. My beautiful bed. Streatly. The gym with its lovely view. The internet. Wifi! Billiard TV. Books. Driving a car. Breakfast by the river.*

## List of Creations You Are Unhappy About
*Example: Did not receive a raise in pay*

*Haven't had a raise (a pound) in years. I was a good girl + didn't complain about it. I don't like dips in the market that deflate the work of my investments.*
*I feel nervous of current market conditions.*
*I don't know whether to bring my rands to the UK.*
*Rands are devaluing quickly!*

Are you willing to embrace one of those creations you are unhappy about in unconditional love each time it occurs until it becomes a creation you consider as wonderful?

## The Concept of Importance

One of the more interesting concepts we have created is that of importance. We give some events, people and concepts more importance than others.

For example: We do not consider having left our wallet at home when we are at the checkout counter of a store as important as having to declare bankruptcy.

Yet, both are events that we have made up. Although they have no reality, they not only seem real, their relative importance also seems real.

Another way of describing importance is the concept of weight—giving something weight. Weight is related to seriousness. We give a lot of importance, weight and seriousness to declaring bankruptcy.

## The Disguise of Importance

The concept of importance and its relatives—weight and seriousness—are disguises for the Beings of Light or Lightness that we are. There is no weight to us. There is no seriousness to us. We are joyful, peaceful and harmonious Beings. Convincing ourselves that we carry weight and that our concepts have weight (importance) is another of our extraordinary accomplishments.

The wonderful opportunity we have is to make light of whatever we consider heavy and to find joy in whatever we consider serious. We do this by first appreciating the extraordinary accomplishment of creating the concepts of importance, weight and seriousness. We are then ready to fully appreciate the light and joyful Beings we really are.

*Exercise*

Pick a belief that you have given importance (weight), then:

1. Feel the heaviness of the belief.

2. Feel appreciation for the creation of the belief.

# CHAPTER 17

# Playing The Money Game

We don't create abundance. Abundance is always present. We create limitation. That is the purpose of the money game.

The way we have designed the game, we keep track of how much money comes in, how much goes out and how much we have left.

We only keep track of something when we believe that the supply is limited. We don't keep track of how much air there is to breathe. We are confident that there is enough air to take our next breath. We don't keep track of how much water comes into our house. We are confident that when we turn on the faucet, water will come out. We don't keep track of how many knives and forks we have. We are confident that when we sit down to a meal, there will be utensils.

The concern we have that leads us to keep track of money is the disguise for the abundance that is our natural state. We can embrace the feeling we call concern as what the feeling really is—the joy of being in the fullness of our abundance.

## CHAPTER 18

# Cost

"There is no free lunch." "You know you'll have to pay for this." "You don't get something for nothing." And, for those in business, "Cost benefit analysis"—is the benefit of having something worth the cost?

We have so convinced ourselves that there is a cost for almost everything that one of the first things we do when we think of having something is to ask, "How much will I have to pay" or "Can I afford this?"

The creation of the concept of "cost" (of having to "pay" for having something) is a very clever way to not only hide the truth of our natural abundance, but also to build in a consequence, a penalty for having something we desire.

When we are in the energy of "cost," or having to "pay" for something, we have the perfect opportunity to embrace that energy as what it really is—the joy of expressing enthusiastic appreciation for constantly being blessed with an infinite flow of abundance that expands with every expression of it.

## CHAPTER 19

# Control

"Get a hold of yourself." "Take control of your life." How often have we heard these statements or ones like them as advice in the form of admonition?

We hear these statements as a reflection of our belief that we are in control of our lives and that we have, for some unknown reason lost control.

What are we attempting to control? We are the Power and Presence of God. We are always in the fullness of peace, harmony, joy and abundance. We don't control this. This is who and what we are.

Then, what is happening when we are having the experience of what we refer to as "taking control?" We are giving ourselves a human experience—something totally different from our natural state.

The belief that we are in control of our lives is an illusion. However, we do have a lot of fun making believe that we are in control.

An example is the way we play with money. This is a game that is based on the belief that we control the flow of abundance in our lives. We work hard to bring money in, avoid letting it go, invest to try to make more, use debt to have more to play with and go bankrupt to be able to start over as we do with a board game.

However, the way we play with money, acting as though we are in control is just a disguise for our natural state of unlimited abundance. When making believe we are in control loses its allure, is no longer fun, we have the opportunity to appreciate that we were never in control of anything.

As the Power and Presence of God, we are infinitely intelligent. This intelligence guides us through our lives. Everything we experience is the perfect experience for us to have. We are always receiving the perfect support. We are always being loved unconditionally by the Universe.

To create our human experiences, we have intentionally convinced ourselves of the opposite—that in order for our lives to work we have to take control.

As we open to accept and trust that we are being led perfectly by our Infinite Intelligence, we'll find that this Intelligence has a great sense of humor. And the belief that we are or ever have been in control of anything is something we can enjoy laughing about.

# CHAPTER 20

# Summary

Money has no power. We are the source of power. We are the creators of everything we experience. Since we are the God Presence, we can only create from the loving, joyful, abundant Beings we are. The disguises we treat as real are intentional creations that allow us to play in the human as limited, fearful and powerless beings.

When we remove the disguises and reclaim our power, our trust in who we really are expands and:

We express who we really are with more freedom and enthusiasm;

We express the fullness of our creativity without any sense of limitation;

We express appreciation for our ever-expanding abundance by generously sharing this abundance;

and

We express the trust that money flows in support of the expression of appreciation.

## CHAPTER 21

# Epilogue

We all create our experiences. You have created this book to support you in expanding your awareness of who you really are and how ingeniously you have hidden this awareness so that your human experience has become possible. You have also created this book to support you in appreciating that you and every one of your creations are extraordinary and wonderful.

There is no limit to your capacity to appreciate. The more you appreciate yourself and your creations in all their aspects, the more magnificent your life becomes.

You are unconditionally loved and supported by the Universe and all in It at all times and under all circumstances. You are free to accept and appreciate as much of this love and support as you wish.

Again, there is one power in the Universe—unconditional love. Vesting this power in people, institutions, events and circumstances—all outside of our-selves—places us at the effect of this power. We be-come the victims of our own imaginary creations. This is the way we have devilishly transformed peace into fear, lightheartedness and joy into gravity, har-mony into opposition and abundance into limitation.

I hope that reading this book inspires you to re-claim your freedom and power to live without limits!

# Further Examples of Expanding Awareness

There are examples of people expanding their awareness and acceptance of their unlimited creative capacity. Reports have described the following:

1. People walking on hot coals without burning the soles of their feet;

2. People breaking planks of wood with their hands and forearms without damage to their bodies; and

3. People bending rebars (steel bars about 3 feet long and 3/4 of an inch in diameter) by walking toward a partner each having the end of a rebar resting in the V at the top of his breastplate and pressing against the front of the throat.

I had the fun of performing the last activity. This was not something I prepared for. I was surprised when offered the opportunity. After seeing another person demonstrate it, I knew I could do it. The knowing filled my consciousness. As my partner and I walked toward each other the rebar bent as though it were a piece of chewing gum.

Performing the above activities does not require a special ability. The belief that we cannot perform these activities requires the same creative power as allowing ourselves to perform the activity.

# Ultimates

## The Ultimate Challenges

Consider what it has taken for us to create the human experience. We start off as the Power and Presence of God, unlimited in all ways. Peace, harmony, joy and abundance are our natural state. And, we accomplish a nearly impossible task. We hide who we really are from our Selves by creating a whole new way of living that is completely opposite to our natural state with personas that are devoid of the power of our real Selves.

## The Ultimate Sleight of Hand

We create this new way of living by making up wild ideas (concepts) such as the money game that is based on our transfer of power to money. Then we spend a huge amount of time trying to retrieve the power by getting our hands on as much money as we can.

## The Ultimate Gift

As the saying goes, "There is method in our madness." Creating the ultimate challenge was a brilliant idea. It has made possible the ultimate gift—living in the human free of the limitations built into the challenge. (Without first creating a human experience of the ultimate challenge, there is no playground in which to enjoy the ultimate gift.)

How do we reach the ultimate gift? By reclaiming the power we placed in concepts such as those that make up the money game.

## The Ultimate Secret

The information that we have to keep hidden from ourselves is our true worth. Our human experience is dependent upon convincing ourselves that we are unworthy. The many disguises we have created are designed to keep our appreciation for our true worth hidden.

## The Ultimate Deception

No matter how successful we are at playing the money game, we always come up short of our true worth. That is proof of the brilliance of the game that we designed as a disguise for appreciating and valuing who we really are.

## The Ultimate Tool

We have retained in our arsenal of power a magic wand—the power of appreciation. Embracing any creation in deep appreciation removes the disguise and frees the energy to be reclaimed as what it really is—unconditional love.

This ultimate game with its ultimate deception is an extraordinary accomplishment deserving of nothing less than our deepest appreciation. As ultimate creators, everything we create is magnificent. Remember it is all in our imagination.

There is no power outside that can diminish our true worth. In fact, there is no one playing the game but our Self—the Oneness, the God Presence that we are.

# Meditations from Grady Claire Porter

## Appreciation

Appreciation is the ever expanding energy of valuing. Appreciation is the joyful expression of acceptance of one's Self as the all in all. In the human, the act of true appreciation is the greatest gift we give ourselves. Affording others the opportunity to appreciate extends and expands this gift.

You are focused on appreciation. You give yourself the opportunity to BE appreciation; to BE the ever expanding energy of valuing your Self and all you create.

You have two words you use often: "Thank You." You give yourself the opportunity now to expand on that expression. First, feel the appreciation for whatever event (and all those in the event) that you create. Feel appreciation for yourself for the creation. Be clear that "Thank You" "I appreciate You" is a conversation with your Self. All those you create in your experience are there to reflect that appreciation back to you.

I have said to you "money's only purpose is to express appreciation" and that is so. That is not a limiting concept of money. Indeed, it is the most expansive energy that we can express and money is delighted to be the tangible expression of that energy.

The opportunity that you have now is to be clear about the vast amount of your Soul power you disguised as money. In setting up a limited economic structure where money had all the power to provide happiness and well being, stature and acclaim (or to take it away) you were able to play the game of limitation and struggle. And now, as you embark on this new game of unconditional appreciation for yourself and that Self that you hid away, you can truly marvel at the unlimited creative being you are and free money up to do what it loves to do: EXPRESS APPRECIATION! As money flows in and out of your experience in joyful appreciation, be clear that it is not the source of your abundance nor is it a measure of it. Be clear that abundance is the infinite, unbounded richness of all we are. Abundance is the essence of our ever expanding experience and expression of appreciation. Money is just one of the infinite number of ways in the human that we create to express appreciation.

I appreciate you.

## The Human Experience

The human experience is but an exercise for the Soul to practice Its perfection. It is not a trivial experience, and many a Soul return to it time and again to master the challenges it offers.

You are that Soul, returned to the human, to practice the perfection of who you truly are. You are that Soul, deeply engrossed in the human, so that your mastery is complete. You are seeing that now.

You are seeing that the events of the human have no real meaning, other than to allow you to experience and accept your mastery. The deep emotional chasms of the human but afford you the opportunity of the deep knowing of your Self. You are seeing that getting involved in the drama of the human events is but the challenge to your Soul Self to remember who you are and why you chose this experience.

We have long shared with each other the concept of human perfection—that it's all perfect, just the way it is. And, the truth of that is evidenced in the creative and magnificent activities you create to practice and experience the reality of your true Self. Let's look at a few:

### *The Body*

In the human, the body represents the identity of an individual, as well as the evidence of its life. No body—no life. You see that this opportunity affords you, the Soul, to experience and practice your eternal manifestation of the infinitely unfolding nature of God, your source. Body size or shape is but a reminder of the formless, powerful energy you are. In the human, you create "norms" or "ideals" around shape and form. Again, what a beautiful and perfect opportunity to express and experience the infinite originality of Self. In the depiction of your creation by God, there is only the recitation of you being made in "God's image" and "Behold, it was very good." In the human, the practice is to look to the manifestation to see what God is like. The practice of the Soul is to look to God to know what the creation truly is.

## *Financial Affairs*

This is one you truly enjoy playing with. In the human, you have adopted what you call "a money-driven society." It takes money to do almost anything, and you have made money a condition for having or experiencing any sense of comfort, security or enjoyment. What a perfect opportunity for the Soul to experience true unconditional love and support. You have always seen a lack of money as somehow a failure on your part to succeed—that you must do something, even in consciousness, to allow money to be a part of your experience. The activity around money is one of the most supportive activities the Soul has in experiencing and expressing Its perfection. One of the most entrenched beliefs set up in the human is that you cannot live without money. And, you have many on the planet acting out that belief. Even more entrenched is the belief that you can solve these peoples' problems with money. I have been attributed as the source of the statement "the poor will always be with you." Well, they will, as long as there is a Soul in the human practicing Its acceptance of full and total abundance. I have said to you, "Money is in total support of you," and it is. Acknowledging, accepting and appreciating your financial affairs, just as they are, opens you to the support of money. Loving, unconditionally, not having money is the activity the Soul creates for Itself. You are that Soul. Your commitment to receive and enjoy bountiful financial abundance is a commitment to loving your current financial abundance just the way it is. You will experience huge amounts of money in your life when money is no longer a condition in your life. You are seeing this; you, as the perfect Soul in the human, are embracing, in deep love and appreciation, all aspects of your financial affairs just as they are. The wealth encountered in that experience is beyond money.

## Relationships

Whether you are relating to your family, a spouse, a lover, a pet, the grocery clerk, your relationships provide the Soul with a wealth of perfect opportunities to practice Its wholeness and completeness. In the human, a "perfect" relationship is revered as a blessing and an accomplishment. The Soul accepts any and all relationships as perfect precisely as they are. The Soul views all relationships as supportive and utilizes the activity of them to practice Its perfection. The Soul knows that the perfect relationship is the one It has with Its Source, and It knows that that relationship is infinite, unconditionally loving and supportive. You are that Soul.

We began this meditation on the perfection of the human experience and the support it is constantly and consistently offering you, the perfect Soul. Acknowledge, accept and appreciate each and every activity of your human experience just as it is. It will not change itself, nor allow you to change it. It will remain precisely as it is to give you the opportunity to do what you came here to do — love it all.

## The Power of Peace

### *The Peace Meditation and the Peace Exercise*

The Peace Exercise is not just an activity. It is a way of life for you from this point on. It is a way to feel the love you have for each part of yourself that you have not yet been ready to unconditionally accept. It is the red carpet for this planet to move forward into absolute joy and harmony. For I tell you this, as you totally and unconditionally love yourself, at all times and under all circumstances, you ARE the High Joy Vibration. And the power of that enlightens the consciousness of whomever and wherever your love and thought are focused.

There are two things that will alert you to begin the Peace Exercise. First, at any time you feel you wish to change ANYTHING OR ANYONE, you are giving yourself the opportunity to experience the power of peace. The second is justification. At any time you feel you must justify anything, to yourself or anyone else, you are telling yourself you are ready to practice the power of peace.

Now be clear on this. Change and justification are not bad. The desire to change and justify is not bad. Both simply come into your experience to support you in doing what you love to do—BEING THE POWER OF PEACE.

### PEACE EXERCISE

*I feel, with unconditional trust, that I am*
*the whole of the Universe, and all that I see is Me.*

*I feel, at my deepest level,*
*the power of being who I am.*

*I feel the willingness and the readiness*
*to exercise the power of being who I am.*

*I feel the gentleness of my own power,*
*and the absolute certainty of knowing*
*that my power is the power of peace.*

*I feel the conviction and trust of my Self so totally
that I no longer need to project anything
but absolute and unconditional love.*

*I feel, in totality, the infinite variety
of my beingness.*

*I feel the warmth and peace of
unconditionally loving my own infinite Self.*

*And, at this deep feeling level,
I this moment yield to the power of my Self,
totally trusting my unconditional love and support
for all of Me, and accept all that I see
as the expression and experience of this power.*

# Universal Principles

Universal Principles are the guidelines that govern our lives perfectly.

## *1. Energy*

The basic component of the Universe, energy, occurs in either materialized or unmaterialized form. All that we see and feel is an expression of energy.

Energy is synonymous with love. When we resist the flow of energy, or love, we experience discomfort. When we align with the energy flowing around us, we feel joyful and at peace.

## *2. Infinite Intelligence, or God*

Within all energy is an intelligence that is infinite, eternal and purposeful. This Infinite Intelligence, which we sometimes refer to as God, or simply love, is the source of all creative expression and the essential power in the Universe.

The way we view our Infinite Intelligence, or God, is precisely the way we experience life. When we perceive God as an unconditionally loving and supportive energy at all times and under all circumstances, we experience our world and everyone in it as totally safe, loving and generous.

### 3. Oneness

Since the essence of everything is pure loving energy, in the truest sense, *we are One.* When we feel our connection to our Oneness, we feel the power of who we really are.

Our Oneness, love, is indivisible. Whenever we attempt to withhold love from anyone, we withhold love from everyone, including ourselves. The truth of this principle becomes clear as we allow our hearts to open and feel our interconnectedness.

### 4. There Is Nothing Outside Of Us

In order to have our human experiences, we created the apparent reality that we are living outside the Oneness; that there are things and people that can affect us without our consent. The truth is that there is nothing outside of us; all that we see is our Self. This becomes our new reality when we open the belief in separation and accept the truth that we are the Power of God.

## 5. Perfection

Our Oneness, God, is perfect and expresses this perfection as unconditional love and support. Whatever unfolds is God happening. When we see other than unconditional love unfolding, we are not seeing clearly. We create unclarity to have the experiences that we came into the human to have.

When we are ready to see with greater clarity, we embrace whatever is before us in unconditional love, trusting that the Universe, in Its constant expression of unconditional love, is sending us the perfect support. With practice, our clarity grows, along with our appreciation for the unconditional love and support that is always present.

## 6. Beliefs

Under the guidance of our Souls, we intentionally adopt the beliefs we hold in order to provide ourselves with the precise experiences we are having. These beliefs help us hide our power so that our journey as humans can unfold as we planned before we entered this realm.

The urge to explore life as a human beyond the limitations of these beliefs is a signal that our Soul Selves are looking to guide us in finding and reclaiming the power we had previously hidden, and to awaken us to the truth of who we really are.

## 7. Intuition, Feelings and Power

Our Infinite Intelligence communicates to us through our intuition, which we access through our feelings. The more willing we are to feel our feelings, the more able we are to connect with the power that resides in them.

The true power in the Universe is a totally peaceful power. It is the power of love, fully, freely and joyfully felt.

## 8. Mutual Support

Our Universe functions as a mutual support system in which each and every thing in existence relates to and affects every other thing. Every person and circumstance in our lives is there to support us by reflecting back to us the present state of our consciousness.

Our creation of the belief that we are naturally competitive and adversarial sets in motion a mirroring back to us of our acceptance of that belief. The more we look for the reflection of our beliefs in each event and circumstance in our lives, the more we appreciate how perfect the Universe's support for us truly is.

## 9. The Mirror Principle

Everything that we see and feel is a reflection of the state of our own consciousness. Every person we attract into our lives is showing us a perception we hold about ourselves.

Every feeling expressed by another mirrors a feeling deep within us.

This reflection is a gift, for it allows us to be aware of the beliefs we hold, and the power that we have hidden in them.

## 10. Nonjudgment

We have carefully taught ourselves to evaluate and judge much of what we experience. However, right and wrong, good and bad are just beliefs, places where we have hidden a lot of our power.

The truth is that everything that occurs is just another event or circumstance. Judging something keeps whatever we judge the way we judge it. Also, judging anyone or anything tells us that we are judging ourselves in the same way.

Judging creates discomfort within us that can only be relieved by opening our hearts, first to the judgment and then to the person or thing we have judged. Expanding this open-hearted energy leads to the joyful feeling of unconditional love for ourselves as the wholeness and completeness of who we really are.

## 11. Purpose

Our Soul knows our purpose for this lifetime and initially supports us by helping us hide our power and our knowing so that we may have the experiences we came here to have. When we are ready to reconnect with our God Presence, our Soul supports us in uncovering our power and our knowing.

We are always on purpose, and we are always a God Presence receiving the perfect support for experiencing and expressing ourselves in accordance with our purpose.

## 12. Comfort and Discomfort

Our bodies are magnificent instruments that we create to support us in having the experiences we come to the human to have. Our bodies are created and maintained in consciousness. They mirror the state of our consciousness, which includes the beliefs in how to look, act, age and die.

Unencumbered by our beliefs, our consciousness is unlimited, as are our bodies. The natural state of our consciousness is perfect ease, as is the natural state of our bodies. The limited beliefs we have about our bodies are there to love and embrace just the way they are. This opens the energy held in the beliefs as it opens the energy in our bodies from that of dis-ease to ease.

## 13. Abundance

Abundance is our natural state as God Presences. Everything we experience is part of the abundance.

When limitation appears, we are seeing a reflection of our beliefs in limitation. Opening these beliefs provides us with a clearer view of our abundance.

### 14. Giving and Receiving

Giving and receiving always occurs in balance. It is as important to receive gratefully, as it is to give voluntarily, generously, and with no expectations. Our willingness to keep the energy flowing in and out of our lives supports the energy in expanding.

The corollary to the principle of giving and receiving is that we give only to ourselves. Since we are all One, when we give to another, we are really giving to ourselves.

### 15. Nonattachment and Freedom

Our perceived need to hold on to anything or anyone demonstrates our beliefs in shortage and personal incompleteness. Holding on to anything—people or possessions—blocks the flow of energy around our experience with the person or object and reduces the joy of the experience. It also inhibits new people and new things from coming into our lives.

As we open our hearts and expand our trust in the natural abundance of the Universe, we give ourselves and everyone else the gift of freedom.

### 16. Expressing Who We Really Are

Each of us has one or more talents we love to express.

When we are fully and freely expressing who we really are, we feel joyful and fulfilled.

The more love we feel for ourselves, the more we allow the creative energy of the Universe to flow through us.

Since how we see and feel about ourselves is how we see and feel about other people, feeling more love for ourselves is the most mutually supportive focus we can have.

## 17. Means and Ends

Means and ends are the same. The action and outcome are one.

To enjoy peace, we feel and express our inner peacefulness. To enjoy a life that works perfectly, we see and feel the perfection of everything and everyone, including ourselves. To enjoy the natural abundance of the Universe, we feel and express gratitude for everything just the way it is.

## 18. Harmony in Relationships

Every relationship in our lives reflects our relationship with our Self. Every person we attract is there to support us in opening our hearts and reclaiming the power of Self-appreciation.

When we feel love for ourselves, and the perfection of ourselves, just the way we are, we attract loving and harmonious relationships with other people.